This Bright Darkness

This Bright Darkness

Sarah McKinstry-Brown

Black
Lawrence
Press

Black
Lawrence
Press

www.blacklawrence.com

Executive Editor: Diane Goettel
Book Design: Amy Freels
Cover Design: Zoe Norvell

Published 2019 by Black Lawrence Press.
Printed in the United States.

Louis Simpson, excerpt from "The Goodnight" from *The Owner of the House:
New Collected Poems 1940-2001*. Copyright © 1959, 2001 by Louis Simpson.
Reprinted with the permission of The Permissions Company, Inc., on behalf
of BOA Editions, Ltd., www.boaeditions.org.

With gratitude to my mom and dad,
for showing me how to love the world
and find the music within it.

Contents

II. Summer

III. Departure

Epilogue

The lives of children are
Dangerous to their parents
With fire, water, air,
And other accidents;
And some, for a child's sake,
Anticipating doom,
Empty the world to make
The world safe as a room.
—Louis Simpson

It's strange that our love of Beauty should lead us to hell.
—Robert Bly

Prologue

Chorus: After 13 Months of Searching, the Girl's Body is Found Five Miles from Our House

Nights we sat down to dinner, interlaced
our fingers and recited The Lord's Prayer,
she was there, taking root, a seed
with his seed inside her.

Abandoned by the sun,
lost in the thick woods
of some man's fever,
we can't stop looking at our daughters.

And when the girl's mother appears
on the evening news, distraught,
but grateful for a body, we understand.

From the deep well of our wombs,
we draw our daughters up,
bring them to our breast,
quench a thirst they didn't know
they had, saddle them with hunger

so they might stay.

Let it not be his hands that claimed her. Let it be
the tender dirt, the earth slowly awakening
to her body as it softens in the sun,
preparing her,

each pearl of larvae working to ease
the burden, to release her
from the body that caught his gaze.

I. Return

Chorus: The Flowers Advise Girls on the Cusp

You can call it rot. Or you can call it rust.
Either way, this story is so old, it's written in dust.

He wants you soft and fecund
until he gets you alone. Then he'll show

the fact of his body; how a man only needs one hand
to circle both of your wrists.

When he flicks his lit cigarette to the ground,
you'll know sorrow

that slow grind of boot heel
against wet earth.

He believes the only way he can harden,
is if you shed your name. (By this we mean to say

he wants you gone, wants you
broken.) Girls, cock your spines and listen:

fear makes the eyes and ears bloom.

Press that black flower to your face.
Learn its scent like your own flesh. Come spring,

let us cover you; let us dress your wounds
with fragrant blooms.

Persephone's Statement

He said my mother had set the whole world
on fire, so what was the difference? I was always

thirsty. He said the body is a ladle. He promised
I would learn to burn beneath his gaze;

that if I closed my eyes
and told him where to put his hands

I'd hear the brook where I used to bathe.
He said the body is a field,

said if I softened beneath him,
the grass above us would green again.

No. I don't sleep. When I dream,
it's always the same

Mother leans in to kiss the top of my head,
and I am pulled under. My hair,

once famous to the sun, gone anonymous,
fused with the old cottonwood's roots.

The world above me is on fire. The rivers are flowing backwards;

the sky is falling; the calves in the fields cannot drink
from their mother's teat, and the grass doesn't remember

green. It's my fault. If I soften beneath him,
he promises the sky. I open.

Demeter's Statement

Why famine? Because you can't set fire
to what's green. Because grief comes
when you're emptied of everything
but longing. Because nothing

could sate me, I had to feed on my imaginings:
the sinewy neck muscles of a husband, hungry,
kissing his wife's sharpened clavicle,

her mouth a sorrowful *O.*
Because I was all alone
and the heart becomes offal
when a mother is told over and over

that her daughter is just another
siren, a warning, a story to be taught.
Because a man's desire, that knot,
is what tends to this rot.

Because I wanted them to know
what it feels like when every prayer is hollow,
nothing but an ask, a bid, a gamble.
I wanted it to be their hands that trembled

as they touched match tip to candle,
trying to drown the hush
of a suddenly empty cradle,
another small mound of fresh dirt
atop the burial plot.

Persephone, Stumbling into Morning

It hurts. The sun. The salted air.
Those red flowers. Their swollen pistils;

the heifer's udder, raw,
dragging on the ground.

The men, their children starved
by Mother's rage, bow

their heads when I pass. When they kiss
the hem of my dress, I call it *reverence*,

but Mother says that when night falls,
these men, hardened by the now rich soil,

turn to their wives
and grin, slide their tongues

over their teeth as they recall
my story, see me bound and writhing

beneath him,
a pale girl hooked and split.

Persephone in a Crowd, Watching a Wedding Procession

What child has patience for symbols,
those gauzy saffron veils, the bride's wrist

in the beloved's grip as he leads her away.

I remember when my own mother
said not to worry. Said I was a child of the gods.

Said I would never endure such a procession.
Said when it was all over

there would be a feast. There would be gifts, that every bride
is given a painted vessel for fetching water.

I was small. I held onto what I was told and carried it.

I did not know that those women disappeared into the hills
singing and returned mute, blood in their mouths, thighs raw

and burning, the cracked vessel in their hands,

all that water, wasted.

Demeter, Watching Persephone at Her Mirror

She slips out of her dress, turns
this way and that, cursing her breasts,

her stomach, her thick thighs.
Her eyes are crushed geraniums, her mouth

a study in sorrow. Hollow girl, full
of echoes. She pushes her food

around her plate, only pretends
to put the spoon to her lips. How

do I tell her that Man's desire is hunger,
and we are built for famine. I know

she is trying to disappear, to transmute
herself into light. Air. But the girl

is my stock. And her flesh,
that tightly woven basket,

is built to carry the weight
of every harvest moon.

Persephone's Appetite

Mother sets down the plate, pushes back my hair,
leans over and whispers into the top of my head,

Eat.

How can she not know that grief
resides in the gut? Black and sweet,

I can't swallow these figs
ripened by sun and air.

The teeth are willing to bite and tear and gnaw,
but the throat, the tongue's betrothed, tightens.

The body begs to be fed, but since returning
I know my blood's already slowed. Like a child

learning its place in this world,
my heart repeats the only word it knows

no, no, no.

Chorus: The Newscasters

Vanished for so long
the disappeared girls always come home

empty, their eyes, boarded up,

their bodies, a series of locked
doors. Their mothers reach for them

and say, with their embrace,
You can climb out now, you're free.

It's spring. We keep insisting
that the sky is falling. And the mothers

keep grinding the coffee beans,
listening to our mourning forecasts

while the fresh-faced neighborhood girls
trudge toward school, peonies

hanging their heads under the weight
of their own blossoming.

Persephone's Guilt

When I close my eyes
I see the bouquet gathered that day.

I try to change it, but the story sticks.
Flowers tumbling from my hands,

shattering, the hyacinths in shards at my feet, slivers
slipping into my fingers when I stoop to gather them.

His want had me trapped in my skin.
When the door moved, it was only, always,

Him. And when he entered, I closed my eyes,
saw the mouths Mother emptied with drought,

hollowed and packed with dirt.
Those voices still tendril into my dreams, whispering,

rain, rain, rain. I wake parched,
hunted by my own name.

Demeter Explains Her Sorrow

When you first disappeared, I wept into my hands
and drowned. I swept our house clean and scoured its walls

with my own screaming. Suffering
the sun's silence, I said nothing, cut

out my tongue and buried it among the lilacs. I watered
my garden of stones until, strand by strand,

I began to tear each hair from my head
to weave a noose. Oh sorrow, sorrow,

buried by my heart, do you know how long
I carried that small bird in my cupped palms?

Persephone Tries to Grasp Barrenness

My mother's grief. It was impossible

to imagine. The leaves turning, falling
underfoot. All that sky caught between branches. *Where*

will the birds nest? I asked. He said I should be glad

that I was not so small. That my fate
wasn't tied to a single drop of rain. As if

I were not tongued to his heart, tied
to my sex. I find myself wishing, not on petals,

but on glistening maggots, what eases the rot,
frees the bones to sing.

Epithalamium (Persephone's Song for the Bride to Be)

Don't pity me.
You are the one

shackled to the sun,
and yours is a life

of shadows.
Maiden, wash away

the memory of a window
that gave you sky.

Strip your tiny bed.
Spin in your white dress,

your stained mouth,
your borrowed name.

Forget the songs
you knew by heart.

When he slips the ring on your finger,

your blue eyes
burned to ash,

you will open your mouth
only to ask

if he is hungry.

Persephone on Wishing for a Baby

What other promise could free me
from those seamless nights,
the black cloth tightly woven?

A woman needs a thing
to measure her days,
so he gifted me an hourglass,

murmured something
about pearls that form
when a grain slips

between the shell's lips.
Waning. Bereft. I watched sand
squeeze through the neck.

Each time I bled
I felt the moon that I could not see,
the world above me
disappearing.

Demeter Tells Persephone About the Night That She, in Her Grief, Disguised Herself as a Nursemaid and Tried to Burn away the Baby's Mortality

When I learned you had been bartered,
body tendered and brokered

by your own father,

I needed something
to keep the pain at bay.

Softened by my anguish,
the mother mistook me for a mortal,

and took me in as nursemaid.
How many nights did I swaddle

and cradle and hum and rock?
Was it hope or misery

that made me circle my lips with ambrosia,
and kiss his tiny mouth

over and over, turning
what was bitter

back to sweet? Hate is practice.
Love is ritual. Thrust

the dull boy into the hearth;
he will shimmer. Hate is practice.

Love is patience. I waited
for both of our hearts to slow,

listened for the sound of blood turning
from black to gold.

Chorus: The Mothers Who Miscarry

Friends appear on our doorsteps with bouquets.
They don't bring asters or daisies from their gardens.

They splurge, instead, on pricey floral arrangements,
knowing a stilted bud or blackened stem,

the hint of fresh dirt or sun,
some glimmer of tiny exposed roots,

a black ant crawling across a single petal—
could crush us. When they gather in the kitchen,

how strange this silence, how even talk of weather

feels dangerous. No one willing to mention
the coming winter, how the light is already beginning to change,

how, *god*, you blink, and the elm's crimson leaves
are underfoot. When someone feeling brave asks

how we're doing, *really?* We spare them.
They don't want to know what we've become,

how the yoga poses and meditations,
the Chinese herbs and affirmations

worry our wombs
into polished stones,

how grief can ruin a body,
so that even prayer,

the simple clasping of hands,
is violence, reminds us

of the daughters who slipped through our fingers,

of all that we were given
but could not hold.

Persephone Watching the Storm Roll In

Teeth on skin, the sky darkens
and everything,

even the tree that branches low to the ground—its bright fruit—

chains me to him.
Split and cleaned of stem and pit,

at the root of every tongue lies a heart,

so I gave it to him. Seasoned by those starless nights
and the heat of limbs, while Mother sat

on her crumbling throne, how easily I turned to kindling,
the whole world trembling above me.

II. Summer

Chorus: The Mothers of Tomboys Explain Crypsis

Your daughter only wants to shop
in the boys section of the department store.
She gravitates

to racks of black t-shirts
covered in videogame characters

anything to camouflage
her breasts, anything to keep her

covered. She believes
her electric blue tennis shoes

are guarantees,
what will keep her

in the middle of summer.
All mulberry-stained fingers

and Popsicle-red-tongued,
she pulls her baseball cap over her eyes,

lowers her voice by a full octave
so the boys will leave her be:

scraped knees, ashen elbows,
bruised shins, up all night

gaming in the basement,
perfecting her character names,

each one some variation on the words
Blaze or *Cosmic*, names meant to consume

expand, set fire to. The way your girl

moves through the world
is practiced; when the boys speak

she knows their tongues are
tuning forks, the only pitch guaranteed

to tilt the earth's axis; she listens
her ears, memorizing those tones
so she can fine-tune her own.

You are her mother. You carried her.
Knowing the weight

of your own body, you watch her
walk through the house, out the door

and down the street with a gait
that silences her hips, their insistence.

She knows the curves of her body
mean the world, in its hunger,

will mistake her for
a bowl, a cup, a thing

built for quenching.
She wants to be free,

the burden of pink bikes, abandoned,
lying on their sides in a field

the inevitability of that news story.

Whistling, she walks down the block
like the world belongs to her

like her body is a thing
that doesn't need taking.

Demeter: on a Mother's Love

When did my embrace become unbearable?
Why must I always call her back?

My voice echoes the surrounding hills,
asking, always asking. Mine is a love

I can only describe as grief, a grief
I can only describe

as hunger. If I could, I would
swallow her whole and insist her back

into darkness, into my womb, that locket, adorned casket,
anything to keep her my *jewel*, my *shine*, my *glint*

of sun. Buried, all those nights she imagined
herself back. And she screams at me, insists she's trapped,

a glimmer of light
locked in her mother's facets.

Demeter, on Her Daughter's Silence

I have flooded these hills
with a green so bright,

it is impossible to step outside
without shielding your eyes.

But inside my home
some strange blight grows.

She punishes me with her eyes.
Her steady gaze, the knife's tip

at my throat. Such discipline,
how she doles out her words

in small bites, generous
with nothing but this practiced

silence. Whatever the girl was fed
has spoiled her tongue.

Whatever the girl was fed
was decadent. The mouth

that kisses my cheek,
whispers the names of the dead

crossing the River Styx.

Persephone, Famished

In his burned house I was incandescent.

Every day he offered me dark bread,
tore an end from the loaf

tried to coax my mouth open.
Knowing my hunger was a trap, a blessing,

I was without morning in the burned house
until I finally saw myself mirrored in his eyes

where everything,

including my own body,
was scorched,
radiant.

Persephone Learns Her Power among Men

When this world was fat with blooms,
the men were whetted and so full of flesh

they forgot their own bones. They marvel now
at their machinery, how ribs rise and fall

with each breath. They look at their empty hands,
and remember each branch stripped of its leaves.

How quickly everything green becomes memory.
Persephone. I pass and they forget my mother—

invoke my name. When I disappeared, these men
unearthed me in their dreams. My black roots, though buried,

gather water unseen.

Persephone Advises Girls on the Cusp

Evenings he summons you to his bed
grab the hair on the back of his head,

and open your legs. How else will you ever
soften the bell's tongue?

Do not turn yourself inside out;
your rage makes you a mirror. No man or God

wants to look at you and see his own reflection.
When you lie with him,

Put your tender mouth to his
and summon that pasture until your insides moisten.

Remember what you were taught
about the succulents; they save up their moisture, hold

a whole season's worth of water inside their skin, drawing
upon it in times of great drought. This is how we stay green.

Chorus: The Mothers Advise Girls on the Cusp

The one who offers
to carry your groceries
or holds the door open,
insisting,

After you, please
could become

the one who asks,
May I? before leading you by the elbow
toward the dance floor
where he, like a good man,

knows the only way to begin
is to spin your body

away from him.
But what if,
good daughters,
you misread your future?

What if the one who offers
to carry your groceries,
or holds the door
open, insisting,

is the one who invites you to his place
and steers you by the elbow

toward an open bottle of wine,
his bedroom door, ajar?
What if he stands, reaches

for your hand, says,
let's dance and spins your body

into him
his cock hard
against your thigh
even as his mouth persists

Just one kiss—that little white lie
flowering behind your ear.

Persephone Tells her Mother about the Moment She and Hades Parted

When he placed the coin on my tongue
and thumbed my eyelids shut,

I softened. I know your world
has come undone.

You need to believe
the truth is a tossed coin,

two sides spinning
in the sun.

You need to believe
that we all fall on one side

or the other. What chasm
would you be forced to cross, if you saw us

lingering at the gates, him holding my gaze
as I turned that fruit round and round

in my palm? What if the hands
that push us into the fire

are the same ones that pick us up
when we fall? Oh Mother.

What choice is there
when we have none at all.

Chorus: The Mothers on the Meaning of Names

What if the hand that slips a ring on your finger
and plants a single bloom inside your womb

gives you a daughter?
Knowing that the girl, born,

will become a woman,
knowing that a man may, someday,

enter her (over and over)
knowing you cannot predict

whether her name
will spill from his mouth—

a prayer, a curse, a fist, a life-sentence—
this daughter of yours,

what, girls,
will you call her?

After a Fight with Her Mother, Persephone Writes Her Best Friend

I tumble from this house,
half-expecting to find him

under the olive tree, beckoning.
I curse the blue air,

and crawl inside my own
weeping, dream this earth

inside out, return to the moment
I told him I was with child.

His eyes, stones,
softened to ash.

Mother says when the leaves threaten to turn,
if I do not speak of my *Hell*

the women will tear me apart.
The light is changing.

The child in me grows strong. Sweet
eclipse. And they said nothing could grow

in darkness.

Demeter, Coming to Grips

In his world, the body is always seasoned. Skin salted by dank heat,
she forgot the dew, your voice, the sun that could not keep her safe.
Refusing her thirst, how many hours did she sit and watch the cup, filled
to brimming, sweat with water? We are all taught to be small—urns
poured and cast to hold what quenches a man's thirst. Now crowned, the
sea he sowed inside her, flutters of a new life. Say it. Your daughter was
swallowed by his hunger. Say it. A woman's staying has nothing to do
with her own appetite.

Persephone, to a Stranger

Touch me take me back
to the center

where I was small
spooled in her arms

answering to nothing
but my hunger.

Touch me till my eyes
roll back, my lids

half-mast. Thrust me in
the middle of June

when grasshoppers
thrum & itch. Let

sun & heat lick each iris
open, touch me take me to

the bottom. Let me become
sun. Stark on your neck,

weeping salt & sweat
touch me touch me

hear me cry, cast your eyes
see how & why

all this green
must wilt & bow

under the weight
of my opening.

Demeter Rages at the Gods

It is easy to love a whisper, a rumor,
a hidden promise, a bulb in winter.

It is something different when the child is born and blooms
at your breast, your hem, your bedside, your back,

her eyes and mouth asking, always
asking. What do you want me to say? That I never

wished her away? That, when I watched her
spinning in the field, the sun tangled

in her hair, I did not curse my own heart?
If a woman tries to run from what binds her

she will fall. Again and again. Fettered,
crawling on her hands and knees. Lullaby,

forget sleep. Bury your dreams.
grind your teeth and weep. Why name the child

before we see its face? Faith? Dumb
grace? Oh Persephone. Persephone.

Demeter Writes Hades

You are no better than the men up here,
all pricks and fists,

smuggling girls into small, dank spaces,
breeding creatures to open

without air or sun or water. Little Flower,
you're small now. You've had her.

This story will turn and you will learn
what us women have always known:

when the mouth kissing yours
is stripped of tenderness,

there is no other loneliness. Orchids and stones
speak the same language.

Demeter's Guilt

Oh Daughter. Fear, like desire, is a splinter embedded in the palm.
If you try to rid yourself of it,

the thing will only move deeper into your flesh.

The fault was mine. I wanted you to bathe in the creek,
to delight in picking hyacinths. Afraid

you'd always look over your shoulder,
I never told you how you were conceived,

how your father, a god who could level mountains with a whisper,
pinned me against a tree, delighted in biting my neck

and using his knee to keep me open. That flower was a snare
planted by your father's hand,

and you were a girl taken
with her own confusion.

The juice that is both sweet and sour
lingering in the back of the throat.

Persephone Resists Her Myth

I'm a sliver of light under a locked door,
a scythe, a parable whispered at bedtime,

my sex, the cure and the curse
that cinches me into this dress fashioned

from shadows, weds me to the moment
I was taken. Stop holding vigil.

Forget me. Let the grass green.
I am not a warning, the siren you sound

when your daughters, under guise of picking flowers,
wander out of earshot, whispering

He loves me. He loves me not.

Demeter Learns Her Story Is Circulating

What good can come of it
if there is no man or God

who will sing her home to me.
No chants or incantations to undo

this gravity; no coin or promise
to spin the earth

and bend this nightmare
back into dream. My eyes are branded

with stars and I will not sleep
until I find out who has written

this ending on them. My daughter's wrists
bound by blood and ink, who will unspeak

his desire, the moment before he was upon her?
When she bowed to pick that flower,

why the sun? Why this hillside shuddering
with gold and green?

Why this endless story?
Whose hands circle our throats
as we sing?

Last Days of Summer: Demeter Insists the Chorus Spread Persephone's Story

Stitch her up, and spin her round,
glaze her eyes, smooth her dress.

Sluice the tongue, tie the bow,
call the children 'round.

This telling
is our only currency.

With the coming winter
we must promise,

What is lost can be found.
The earth will again green, soften.

And I, oh I,
must try not to wail and keen

when we get to the part of the story,
where my daughter

places the coins
over her own eyes

and lies back in the grass
to die.

Chorus: The Grandmothers Speak

This is the season of unraveling.
Your daughters will change, go from bright yellow

to whispers, and nothing will keep them
from disappearing. We see this end coming, see

how easily it takes them. They learn to walk,
then ride a bike, then turn the keys of the ignition,

the pitch of your voices as you call out,
Wait, Child! Wait for me! verging

on something ugly.

No matter how far you run, you will not reach them
as they round this bend. Your daughters' hair trailing,

catch a last glimpse of the girls you once knew.
You know how this must end. Breathless,

the sun rises. The story
begins again.

III. Departure

Persephone Lets the Blind Beggar Read Her Palm

He says we are kindred, and because his gaze
has the look of forever, I believe him. I say, *You are not blind.*

It is men, bound by vision, who are always groping,
desperate to devour the world

with their hands. He slides his thumb along
my palm and murmurs, *We both live in a world*

of shadows, and I break, fall to my knees,
grasp the hem of his robe,

my sobs shaking the earth,
stripping the orchards of their fruit.

I am tired of looking up.

My heart was not built to carry. His want. Her sorrow.
The sun slides further down the horizon.

Everything sweet
has fallen.

Demeter, on Hope

I settle my gaze on dust trapped in beams of sun,
and marvel at its frenzied spinning, its silence.

The door I believed would never shut,
is closing, my daughter's bright voice humming

on the other side. It is my turn to listen and wait, to want
as I taste the tears that lingered in the corners

of my own mother's mouth. I sip my wine
and stare at the clipped violet placed in a vase

with just enough water to keep from dying.
The women plant bulbs in their gardens,

and all I can see is another thing
that will need tending.

Demeter Prepares Persephone for Departure

What is this curious ritual? She lives,
and I prepare her for burial. I bathe her,

massage oil of the olive into her skin,
braid baby's breath into her hair,

the two of us weeping. Tomorrow
I will watch her walk toward the rising sun

until she disappears, swallowed by that field of clover.
This is a burden I do not know how to shoulder.

What mother is tasked with watching her daughter
die over and over?

Persephone Says Goodbye to Her Mother

Let me go.

Watch me from the window.

Look for me in the ivy climbing the trellis,
the black berries that ripen

in winter. Blind, reaching,
don't let us be like men,

arms outstretched, insisting
a woman cannot make her way

in such darkness. I know now that love without loss
dulls us. When the women

lead their fattened cattle to the shed,
the sharpened blade is kindness.

Demeter Watches Her Daughter Walk Away

Longing for what I cannot touch
feeds a madness that makes me too much like men.

Best to release the rope, and forget how to swim; best to sink
to the bottom and stay there until the sun

becomes a myth, a marvelous lie, the lullaby

all mothers will hum as they tuck in their daughters.
The hills green and clamoring,

my daughter's name strewn like seed to feed the gaggle,
the girls who must be kept

from wandering. I've wailed, I've wailed for so long
when will these cries turn to song?

Demeter: On the Eve of the First Frost

What no one tells you about loss
is that your wishes become small.

I keep what she left behind:
cuttings, a handful of wilted petals,

a locket of hair, an eyelash, the cup
where her lips last lingered as we breakfasted,

her mouth stained the deep red
of cherries. The delphinium she gathered

all those months ago

have turned from red, to blue, to ash.

Demeter, First Snow

I gave my whole life
to softening. My body, my soil,

loosening and turning itself over
to bed the seed of every creature's hunger.

No matter how long the harvest, how sharp
the till,

someone always goes hungry.
Someone

always wants more.

Demeter, Cleaning House

I lean into my broom and stare out the window,
watch the setting sun's slow, honeyed
rhythm. *When she labors, who will loosen*
her braid? Who will speak the words

to smooth the knot in her brow? Worn down with worry,
I wonder, *When did I become so like them—*
those sad women hollowed out.
Who will light the myrrh, wormwood and garlic

to soften the womb's mouth? My view,
unbroken, I remember the field of poppies
gone to seed and bleeding. I see, now, these
dark openings. How each flower

is a reckoning, a possibility. All the ways
this world designed to take her from me.

Epilogue

Chorus: The Searchers

In this field

a sliver of ribbon or strand of hair
is miraculous, what might deliver us

from our sleepless nights, hours
spent locked inside the pitiful dark room

of our imaginings. We walk
deliberately. Head down,

one foot in front of the other,
this is the closest to god

we've ever been. With hands
we forget our bodies,

their ravenous appetites.
We believe, finally,

in what can't be seen,
our vision tuned so taut

each blade of grass sings.
We've been versed

in decay, told that a body,
no matter how small,

can't stay sweet
if left for too long.

Look how,
with every passing hour,

we sweep the land,
our grid search

opening the acres
before us:

a window, unlatched
a door, unlocked

a voice, unhinged.
Watch the mouth, that hollow,

become the bottom of a well,
when a man near the creek bed calls out

before falling to his knees.
Come dusk. Come darkness.

Our heads raise
just in time to see

a chorus of birds, startled
from the trees,

lifting.

Acknowledgements

Thanks to the editors of the following publications where these poems, sometimes in different form, first appeared:

"After 13 Months of Searching, the Girl's Body is Found Five Miles from Our House" originally appeared in *Cradling Monsoons*. San Francisco: Blue Light Press, 2010.

"Persephone's Thirst" and "Demeter Rages at Persephone, Part II." *The Briar Cliff Review.* Spring (2015).

"Persephone, Stumbling into Morning," "Persephone & Demeter Reunited," "Persephone Resists Her Myth." *burntdistrict*. Winter (2014).

"Demeter, Watching Persephone at Her Mirror." *Green Mountains Review Online.* December 19. 2016.

"Demeter, on Hope," "Demeter Prepares Persephone for Departure," "Persephone Says Goodbye to Her Mother," "Demeter Watches Her Daughter Walk Away," "Demeter: On the Eve of the First Frost," "Demeter: First Snow," "Chorus: The Mothers Comfort Demeter." *HOUSEGUEST* #8. November (2016).

"Demeter's Statement," "Chorus: The Newscasters," and "Chorus: The Mothers of Tomboys Explain Crypsis." *Smartish Pace*, Issue 24 (Feb, 2017).

"Persephone in a Crowd, Watching a Wedding Procession," "Persephone Learns Her Power Among Men," "After a Fight with Her Mother, Persephone Writes Hades," "Persephone Advises Girls on the Cusp," "Demeter Tries to Make Peace with Her Daughter," and "Chorus: The Mothers Advise Girls on the Cusp." *South Dakota Review.* Volume 52, Issues 3-4.

"Epithalamium (Persephone's Song for the Bride to Be),"
"Persephone's Guilt," "Persephone Tries to Grasp Autumn," and
"Persephone, Watching the Spring Storm Roll In." *Sugar House Review*. Spring/Summer (2015).

"Demeter Explains Her Sorrow." *Tinderbox Poetry Journal*. Volume 2, Issue 5.

Thank you, Tracy Baker, for refusing to let me give up on this project. You spent time with these poems and convinced me they mattered when they were still gestating and didn't quite know what they wanted to be. I am grateful. Liz Beischel, you read my manuscript (and ALL my other projects) with the attention and joy of a reader plus the support of a dear, lifelong friend. I love you. Thank you, Julia Anders, for unconditionally loving me since the day we met. Thank you Liz Kay, for your unending friendship, your brilliant mind, and your fierce heart, all of which I called on again during the writing of this book. I'd still be freefalling if it weren't for all of the metaphorical ledges you've talked me down from. Without you this book would not exist. Thank you Jen Lambert for reading the manuscript during your daughter's volleyball game and calling me immediately afterwards to ask ALL the right questions. Natalia Treviño & Stephanie Johnson & aforementioned Crew: All of the Polos, text threads, and emails about the rejections and acceptances, along with the bakeries we might open and the pies we might bake, gave me the laughter and the levity I needed when writing this book. Thank you for your joy & for *your* stories and poems. Thanks to Rebecca Rotert for reading this book early on and recognizing the risks these poems were taking; the fact that you embraced and acknowledged my fears surrounding the work was a great comfort during a time when I needed it most. Thanks to Ellen Struve for your magnificent, necessary playwriting, and for your willingness to read this manuscript back to me in its earliest stages so that I might hear the voices, the music, and the possibilities embedded in my own words as echoed back to me in your beautiful rendering. Kristin Walrod: you are a window and a mirror in my life, always pointing me to new ways of seeing when I need it most, while acknowledging all the beautiful and difficult pieces that make me who I am. Genevieve Williams, thank you for editing this manuscript early on and being the new eyes I needed, again, and again (and again) as I worked to make these poems do what I wanted them to do. I'd like to also acknowledge Marion Stuenkel, my Fairy Godmother who, every-day, helps me figure out how to turn my metaphorical pumpkins into carriages (and vice-versa, when the situation demands).

I must acknowledge those artists who have mentored me directly and through their work: Deep bow to Natasha Trethewey and my Bread Loaf Workshop Cohort, whose time, attention, and grace pointed me to exactly what I needed to do to finish this book. Bill Trowbridge and Teri Youmans Grimm, you've been with me from the beginning, and I couldn't think of better mentors, now friends, to have as I travel this strange world of poetry. To Stacey Waite & Lisa Lynne Moore: Thank you for writing words that managed to contain the whole world of this book within them—your blurbs are humbling. Tom Paine, thank you for pushing me to apply to Bread Loaf—the place where this book finally figured out what it wanted to be. Thank you Lisa Sandlin, Todd Robinson, Miles Waggener, Jerry Cederblom, John T. Price, Jody Keisner, Maggie Christensen, Tammie Kennedy, my TA Cohort, and everyone at UNO, whose support, mentorship, and acknowledgement enable me to continue to do the work I so love.

Michael Hollins, Stephanie Plummer, Chris Hochstetler, Jenny Patrick, and Andrew Bauer: Together we grew and tended to a beautiful reading series at KANEKO. I adore all of you. Thanks, too, to Amplify Arts (formerly OCI) for supporting me, and working artists like me, for close to a decade. Thank you to Nancy Engen-Wedin at the Lied Center for Performing Arts, for all the work you do to bring the arts to underserved populations and for providing me protected time, space, and guidance to grow as an Arts Integration Teaching Artist. Thanks to the Kimmel Harding Nelson Center for the Arts, for awarding me the two-week residency that birthed this book. Thanks, too, to The Nebraska Arts Council for their generous award. To Pete Fairchild, Kristin Fogdall, Scott Stubbs, and all of the talented, kind folks I met at Sewanee: Thank you for being the voices urging me forward as I move toward the next book/adventure. To my husband, Matt Mason, I love you. You've made my life a poem. None of this would exist without you. And, finally, to Carolyn Forché: You don't know me, but I am forever indebted to you for putting your pen to page the year I was born and writing the single image that, some 20 years later, I'd read in *A Country Between Us* and decide that I needed to devote my life to reading and writing poetry with the hope that I might, someday, write a just one line as beautiful and haunting as "bells/waiting with their tongues cut out/for this particular silence."

Photo: Debra Kaplan

Born and raised in Albuquerque, New Mexico, Sarah McKinstry-Brown earned her MFA from the University of Nebraska at Omaha and is the recipient of a Tennessee Williams Scholarship in Poetry from the Sewanee Writers' Conference, two Nebraska Book Awards, and an Academy of American Poets Prize. Author of *Cradling Monsoons*, her poems appear in *RATTLE*, *Ruminate*, *Smartish Pace*, *South Dakota Review*, *Sugar House Review*, and elsewhere. Sarah lives in Omaha with the poet Matt Mason and their two wicked-smart daughters.